DK WORKBOOKS

3rd Grade

Language Arts

Author Anne Flounders

Penguin Random House

DK London
Editors Elizabeth Blakemore, Camilla Gersh
US Editor Margaret Parrish
Managing Editor Christine Stroyan
Managing Art Editor Anna Hall
Senior Production Editor Andy Hilliard
Senior Production Controller Jude Crozier
Jacket Design Development Manager Sophia MTT
Publisher Andrew Macintyre
Associate Publishing Director Liz Wheeler
Art Director Karen Self
Publishing Director Jonathan Metcalf

DK Delhi
Project Editor Neha Ruth Samuel
Editor Rohini Deb
Art Editor Jyotsna Julka
Assistant Art Editor Radhika Kapoor
Managing Editors Soma B. Chowdhury, Kingshuk Ghoshal
Managing Art Editor Govind Mittal
DTP Designer Anita Yadav
Senior Jacket Designer Suhita Dharamjit
Jackets Editorial Coordinator Priyanka Sharma

This American Edition, 2020
First American Edition, 2014
Published in the United States by DK Publishing
1450 Broadway, Suite 801, New York, NY 10018

Copyright © 2014, 2020 Dorling Kindersley Limited
DK, a Division of Penguin Random House LLC
20 21 22 23 24 10 9 8 7 6 5 4 3 2 1
002-197344-Jun/2020

A catalog record for this book is available from the Library of Congress.
ISBN 978-1-4654-1740-4

DK books are available at special discounts when purchased in bulk
for sales promotions, premiums, fund-raising, or educational use.
For details, contact: DK Publishing Special Markets,
1450 Broadway, Suite 801, New York, NY 10018
SpecialSales@dk.com

Printed and bound in Canada

All images © Dorling Kindersley Limited
For further information see: www.dkimages.com

For the curious

www.dk.com

Contents

This chart lists all the topics in the book.
Once you have completed each page, color in
a star in the correct box below. When you have
finished the book, sign and date the certificate.

FACTS

Two words can be placed together to make one compound word.

Read the clues. Then unscramble the letters to reveal the compound word that answers the clue.

Joe's daughter's baby boy (nosndrag) ....

Needs oars to move across water (wortoab) ....

Brown boxes may be made of this (darcdraob) ....

Red, orange, yellow, green, blue, violet, indigo (wbonair) ....

A place to dig and play (xbodans) ....

A sack for school supplies, carried on both shoulders (kacpkacb)

....

Carries astronauts or aliens (pihescaps) ....

A bird that makes holes in trees (rekcepdoow) ....

A sea creature with no bones (hsifyellj) ....

Hot breakfast cereal (laemtoa) ....

A concrete noun names something that can be recognized with the senses. An abstract noun names a concept that cannot be recognized with the senses.

Circle the fish that show abstract nouns.

FACTS

Homophones are words that sound alike but have different spellings and meanings.

In each sentence, a pair of homophones is given. Underline the correct homophone to complete each sentence.

I am allowed / aloud to walk to the library alone.

Holly was to / too tired to go on the hike.

The dog's fir / fur was soft and silky.

Have you heard / herd the weather forecast?

A penny is worth one cent / sent.

If you put a lock on your bike, no one will steal / steel it.

There is not much traffic on our road / rode.

Our dog ate the hole / whole pie when we weren't looking.

The driver pressed the brake / break pedal to stop the car.

I knew / new how the movie ended before I saw it.

Use capitalization for the first, last, and major words in titles.

Draw a line under the letters that should be capitalized in each book title.

the adventures of tom sawyer

alice in wonderland

little house on the prairie

the book of fables

big red

charlotte's web

a bear called paddington

the jungle book

the lion, the witch, and the wardrobe

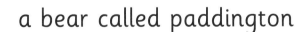

Myths have been created by people of all cultures to explain their history and the ways of the world.

Read the myth, and then answer the questions.

Pandora's Box: A Greek Myth

Zeus, the king of all the Greek gods, was angry at Prometheus for giving the people of Earth fire without asking for his permission. Zeus asked Hephaestus, the god of craftsmanship, to make a beautiful woman from clay. Hephaestus made the woman, and she was named Pandora.

Zeus sent Pandora to live among the people of Earth as Prometheus's brother's wife. Before Pandora left, Zeus gave her a small, locked box. He made her promise never to open it. Zeus expected Prometheus and his brother to be so curious that they would want to open it.

Of course, Pandora was curious, too. The longer she held the box, the more unbearable it became not to know what was in it. Finally, Pandora could not stand it a moment longer. She opened the box.

Out flew all the evils now known to humanity. Crime, rage, disease, war, envy, and hatred came swarming out of the box. Pandora tried to contain them, but it was too late. They were out in the world.

Pandora cried out to her husband for help. They peered into the box together, and it was empty, except for one tiny, glowing creature. The creature climbed out of the box and flew away. That last creature was hope.

What does this myth explain?

....

Why do you think the myth ends the way it does?

....

FACTS

Characters in a story have their own unique traits, thoughts, feelings, and motivations.

Reread the story of Pandora's Box. Then complete the trading cards for two of the main characters in the story: Pandora and Zeus.

Greek Myth Trading Cards

Zeus

Zeus

Who he is: ....

Describe him ....
in two words: ....
What he did: ....

....

Why he did ....
what he did: ....

Pandora

Pandora

Who she is: ....

Describe her
in two words: ....
What she did: ....

....

Why she did
what she did: ....

Writing a letter is a great way to communicate information and ideas to another person or people. A letter is set up to show clearly whom the letter is from and when it was written.

Read about how to write a letter below.

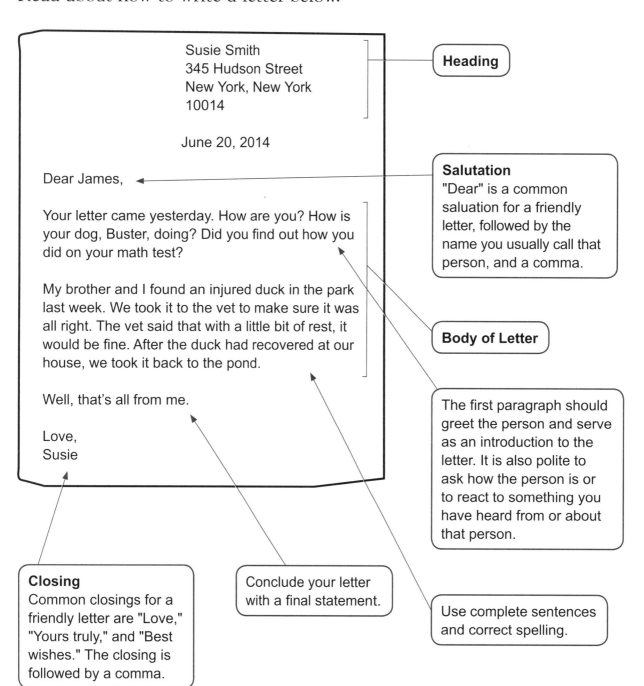

Susie Smith
345 Hudson Street
New York, New York
10014

June 20, 2014

Dear James,

Your letter came yesterday. How are you? How is your dog, Buster, doing? Did you find out how you did on your math test?

My brother and I found an injured duck in the park last week. We took it to the vet to make sure it was all right. The vet said that with a little bit of rest, it would be fine. After the duck had recovered at our house, we took it back to the pond.

Well, that's all from me.

Love,
Susie

Heading

Salutation
"Dear" is a common saluation for a friendly letter, followed by the name you usually call that person, and a comma.

Body of Letter

The first paragraph should greet the person and serve as an introduction to the letter. It is also polite to ask how the person is or to react to something you have heard from or about that person.

Closing
Common closings for a friendly letter are "Love," "Yours truly," and "Best wishes." The closing is followed by a comma.

Conclude your letter with a final statement.

Use complete sentences and correct spelling.

A letter has a specific structure. A friendly letter would be written to family or friends.

Write a friendly letter to a friend or relative to share what you have been doing lately.

....
(Your name)

....
(Your street address)

....
(Your city, state, and zip code)

....
(Today's date)

....

....

....

....

....

....

....

....

....

....

(Your signature)

★ Verb Tenses

FACTS

A verb is a word that names an action or a state of being. Verbs can describe what is happening in the present, the past, and the future.

Underline the correct form of the verb for each sentence.

My mother drives / will drive me to school tomorrow.

I hear an owl hooted / hooting in the distance.

Charlie can play / played the tuba very well.

Jess likes / will like to write poetry, and she is very good at it.

The snake just slithering / slithered into the hollow log.

The teacher is repeating / repeated the directions for the students who are confused.

Look at Yoshi dribble / dribbled the basketball down the court!

I figure / will figure out the answers when I have time.

Maria deposits / deposited the money in the bank yesterday.

Liam screamed / will scream when he bang / banged his knee on the table.

The different forms of a verb are called tenses.

Complete the table to describe the robot's activities.
Write each verb shown in its other two tenses.

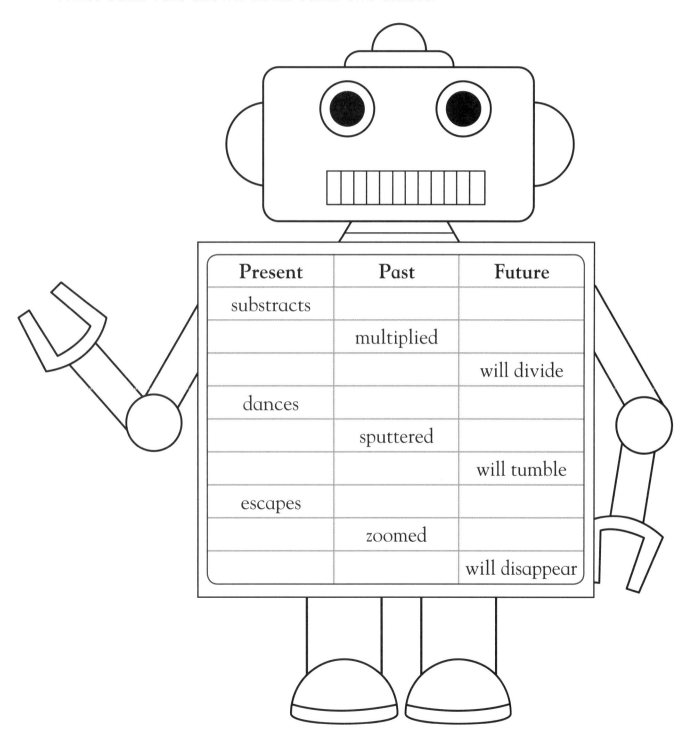

Present	Past	Future
substracts		
	multiplied	
		will divide
dances		
	sputtered	
		will tumble
escapes		
	zoomed	
		will disappear

With regular verbs, the past tense is formed by adding **-ed** to the end of the verb. Verbs that don't play by that rule are called irregular verbs.

The following verbs are irregular verbs written in the simple past tense. Write the present tense verb for each.

Past	Present
felt	
bet	
put	
chose	
gave	
swam	
left	
stung	
caught	

Write two versions of a sentence for each verb pair. Use the present tense in one and the simple past tense in the other.

rise/rose ....   sweep/swept ....

....

sit/sat ....   bring/brought ....

....

FACTS

> When writing the words that people say, surround the words with quotation marks.

Place commas and quotation marks as needed in the following sentences.

I will help you clean up I said to my dad.

Jamie said I can't find my homework.

Max asked Do you want to ride bikes with me?

All you need is love sang the Beatles.

The coach shouted Get into your positions!

My dog has fleas sighed Ben.

When is the next train to New York leaving? I asked.

Here I am! I exclaimed.

You need to floss your teeth every day
the dentist explained.

The teacher asked How many eggs are in a dozen?

FACTS

Some English words are formed from root words that come from ancient languages such as Greek and Latin.

Look at the illustrations. Each illustration shows a word made up of two root words. Find the root words in the root bank that make up each word. Write the word. Then write a definition for the word.

cycle (wheel, circle)	hemi (half)	uni (one)	phone (sound)
sphere (globe, ball)	tele (far, away)	thermo (heat)	meter (measure)

....
....
....

....
....
....

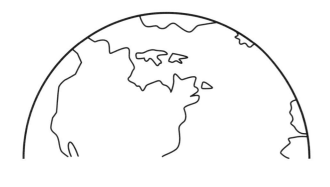

....
....
....

....
....
....

Main Idea and Supporting Details

The main idea is the most important information that the writer wants the reader to know. Main ideas are explained or proven with supporting details.

Read the paragraph. Write the main idea and three supporting details in the space provided.

All animals are different, but platypuses are particularly unusual animals. They look like a mixture of many other animals. They have flat tails like beavers. They have thick fur that is well suited to water like otters. They have bills and webbed feet like ducks. Their webbed feet have claws, so they are able to dig and to swim. Platypuses are also unusual because they are venomous mammals. A male platypus can sting other creatures to defend himself. Finally, platypuses are one of the only mammals that lays eggs.

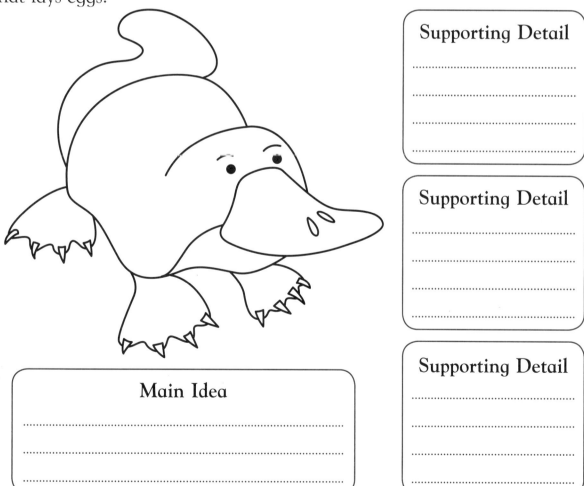

Supporting Detail

....
....
....
....

Supporting Detail

....
....
....
....

Main Idea

....
....
....

Supporting Detail

....
....
....
....

FACTS

Myths have been created by people of all cultures to explain the history and the ways of the world.

The Heron and the Hummingbird: A Native American Myth

The birds Heron and Hummingbird both loved fish. They worried that there were not enough fish to satisfy them both. One day, Hummingbird said, "Let us race to the old tree at the end of the river. The bird who sits on top of the tree first will win. The winner of the race will own all the fish in the waters."

Heron agreed. The birds began their race the next day. The tree was a long way off, so they knew it would take some days to reach it. Heron moved slowly but steadily. His great wings made huge, quiet flaps. Quick little Hummingbird flew this way and that. He flew to all the pretty flowers he saw, stopping quickly to taste their nectar. If Heron got ahead of him, Hummingbird would zoom past him. By nightfall, Hummingbird was very tired. He fell asleep. Heron kept going, softly flapping his wings through the night.

This went on for three days and nights. When Hummingbird woke up on the fourth day, the tree was in sight. Heron was not, so Hummingbird excitedly zoomed ahead to win the race. When he arrived at the tree, he saw Heron sitting at the top. Heron had not stopped to sleep at all during the race. While Hummingbird was the faster flyer, he had stopped at too many flowers and taken too many naps.

From that day on, Heron has owned all the fish in the waters. Hummingbird could no longer fish, so he took his meals from the flowers he loved, stopping at each colorful blossom to sip its nectar.

Describe Heron. ....
....

Describe Hummingbird. ....
....

What does this myth explain? ....
....

The first person is written from the point of view of the main character or the author. The third person is told from the point of view of an outside observer.

Determine whether each passage below is written in the first person or the third person. Circle the correct answer.

Every fall, I am amazed when the leaves on the trees turn bright colors.

first person   third person

The bear curled up inside the hollow log. He got himself ready for the long, sleepy winter.

first person   third person

When I heard the alarm buzzing, I knew it was time to roll out of bed.

first person   third person

The barber asked Dan, "Just the usual cut today?" Dan wondered if he should try something new.

first person   third person

Write a sentence in the first person. ....

....

Write a sentence in the third person. ....

....

FACTS

A timeline shows the order of events in history.

Look at the timeline. Then answer the questions.

Submarine (1776)
Allowed underwater exploration and defense

Steamboat (1807)
Allowed people to travel up and down rivers

Telegraph (1844)
Let people communicate immediately across long distances

Typewriter (1873)
Helped people create easy-to-read documents

Lightbulb (1879)
Made electric lighting inside the home possible

1770   1800   1830   1860   1890

Cotton gin (1794) Helped people to clean and process cotton, allowing cotton to become a major crop in the United States

Sewing machine (1833)
Helped people sew many garments and other items quickly

Telephone (1876)
Allowed clear spoken communication across distances

Of the inventions shown on the timeline, which invention was the earliest?

....

Of the inventions shown on the timeline, which invention was the latest?

....

Which was invented first: the telegraph or the telephone?

....

Name one invention that helped people communicate better.

....

Name one invention that helped people travel better.

....

Cause is the reason something happens.
Effect is what happens as a result of the cause.

In each sentence, draw one line under the cause.
Draw two lines under the effect.

After the phonograph was invented, people were able to listen to music at home.

The invention of the elevator allowed people to construct tall skyscrapers in cities.

Cleaning cotton by hand was a slow process, and many cotton seeds were lost.

Cotton could be cleaned quickly with the invention of the cotton gin.

Write each cause and effect as one complete sentence.

Cause: People used to burn candles for light at home.
Effect: There were many house fires.

....

....

Cause: People needed a safer source of light for their homes.
Effect: Thomas Edison worked on inventing the lightbulb.

....

....

Cause: Thomas Edison invented the lightbulb.
Effect: People could safely use electricity to light their homes.

....

....

★ Prefixes

FACTS

Adding a prefix to the beginning of a word changes the meaning of the orignal word.

Look at each set of words. Based on the meanings of the words, write what you think each prefix means.

agree   disagree
appear   disappear

Dis- means ....

read   misread
spell   misspell

Mis- means ....

fill   refill
send   resend

Re- means ....

possible   impossible
proper   improper

Im- means ....

kindergarten   prekindergarten
historic   prehistoric

Pre- means ....

Adding a suffix to the end of a word changes the meaning of the original word.

Look at each set of words. Based on the meanings of the words, write what you think each suffix means.

care   careful
pain   painful

-**ful** means   ....

care   careless
fear   fearless

-**less** means   ....

bake   baker
teach   teacher

-**er** means   ....

low   lowest
high   highest

-**est** means   ....

big   bigger
small   smaller

-**er** means   ....

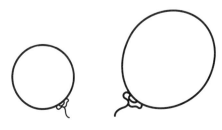

FACTS

The subject of a sentence tells who or what the sentence is about. The simple subject is usually a single noun. The predicate of a sentence tells what the subject is or does. The simple predicate is usually a single verb.

Draw one line under the subject of each sentence.
Draw two lines under the predicate of each sentence.
Circle the simple subject and the simple predicate.

Erica knitted a wool scarf.

My grandfather collects toy trains.

Jason went to the beach.

The fluffy cat stretched its legs.

Minnesota has many lakes.

The crooked swing hangs from the tree.

The jolly farmer sang while he worked.

The soccer fans shouted loudly when their team scored.

Sally Ride was the first American woman in space.

The capital of Colorado is Denver.

Sometimes a sentence can have a compound subject, or more than one subject. A sentence can also have a compound predicate.

Read each sentence. Determine whether the underlined part of each sentence is a compound subject or a compound predicate. Some sentences have both! Circle the correct answer.

<u>John **and** Tara</u> enjoy swimming in the summer.

Compound subject | Compound predicate | Both

Mary <u>opened her locker **and** looked for her science book</u>.

Compound subject | Compound predicate | Both

The train <u>will stop in Philadelphia **and** continue on to Baltimore</u>.

Compound subject | Compound predicate | Both

<u>Tom **and** his dad</u> went fishing in the creek.

Compound subject | Compound predicate | Both

<u>Jack **and** Mary</u> spoke with the teacher and the principal.

Compound subject | Compound predicate | Both

<u>Birds **and** butterflies</u> <u>are pretty to see **and** help flowers grow</u>.

Compound subject | Compound predicate | Both

<u>The actors **and** the dancers</u> <u>performed wonderfully **and** made the audience clap and cheer</u>.

Compound subject | Compound predicate | Both

FACTS

Poems are made up of lines. Lines grouped together in a poem are called a stanza.

Read the poem. Then answer the questions.

Little Things
By Ebenezer Cobham Brewer

Little drops of water,
Little grains of sand,
Make the mighty ocean
And the pleasant land.

Thus the little minutes,
Humble though they be,
Make the mighty ages
Of eternity.

How many stanzas does this poem have?

....

What concrete nouns are in the poem?

....

In which stanza do you find the concrete nouns?

....

What abstract nouns are in the poem?

....

In which stanza do you find the abstract nouns?

....

Why do you think the title of this poem is "Little Things"?

....

Underline the words that make the poem rhyme.

Poems are pleasing to the ear. They can be written with rhythm and rhyme.

Try writing an eight-line poem of your own. It can be about anything you like: a feeling, something in nature, or a favorite activity or pet. Use the structure of the poem "Little Things" on page 26.

Title: ....

....

....

....

....

....

....

....

....

....

....

....

....

★ Apostrophes

Apostrophes can be used to show possession.

Read the passage. Add apostrophes for possession where they are needed.

Sarahs cat had three kittens. As Sarah stroked the kittens soft heads, she thought, "How will I find homes for all of my cats kittens?"

Sarah made posters to put up in her neighborhood. She also hung some in her friend Lindsays neighborhood.

Lindsays dad, Mr. Smith, called Sarah. "Next weekend is my brothers birthday," he said. "He has agreed that a kitten would be a wonderful present."

Sarah was happy to find a home for one of the kittens. She lifted a gray-and-white kitten out of its basket. She walked with it to the Smiths house.

Later, Sarahs neighbor called. "Our house has been lonely since my husbands dog ran away," she said. "We would love to take two kittens."

The kittens new homes were perfect.
Everyone was happy.

adwcskfbomhqanwscjgikeyz

> Apostrophes are used when making contractions. A contraction takes two words and forms them into one.

Make contractions from the underlined words.

<u>I would</u> like to go home.   ....

Susan <u>cannot</u> figure out how to use her MP3 player.   ....

I think <u>you will</u> like this movie.   ....

My dog <u>does not</u> come when he is called.   ....

I <u>would have</u> taken the bus, but I missed it.   ....

<u>It is</u> going to snow later today.   ....

<u>We are</u> paddling in a canoe.   ....

<u>Here is</u> the cake I baked!   ....

You <u>must not</u> make noise when the baby is sleeping.   ....

<u>You have</u> got spinach in your teeth.   ....

They <u>are not</u> following the directions.   ....

<u>They are</u> not following the directions.   ....

Silent Consonants

FACTS

Some consonants are silent in the spelling of a word.
They are written, but not pronounced.

Meet the silent consonants. You'll never know they're there, unless you know how to spell the word. Match the words from the word bank to each silent consonant. Write the matching words on each silent consonant's briefcase. **Hint**: One word has two silent consonants.

write	neighbor	plumber	right	straight	knight	knife
	crumb	knot	wrong	thumb	who	
knee	doubt	high	dough	wrist	lamb	know

silent B   **silent GH**   **silent K**   **silent W**

Look-Say-Cover-Write-Check

A great way to learn how to spell words is the look-say-cover-write-check method.

Look at the words. Say the words aloud. Cover the words. Then write the words. Check your work against the word list.

Word	First Try	Second Try	Third Try
blueberries			
cheapest			
climber			
delightful			
discover			
earring			
fairly			
neighbor			
rewrite			
safer			
scarecrow			
shadow			
telephone			
wireless			
wreck			

★ | Adjectives

To compare two nouns, you can use a comparative adjective. When comparing more than two nouns, you can use a superlative adjective.

Write the comparative form of the adjectives.

The Missouri River is (long) .... than the Mississippi River.

The drums were (loud) .... than the other instruments in the band.

I feel (good) .... than I did when I woke up this morning.

My cat's fur is (soft) .... than my dog's fur.

Your joke is (silly) .... than the one I told.

Winter seems (dark) .... than any other season.

The book I just read has a (happy) .... ending than the last book I read.

Write the superlative form of the adjectives.

My uncle is the (tall) .... member of my family.

Robert is the (quiet) .... child in the class.

Ms. Gray is the (busy) .... person I know.

The blue whale is the (large) .... animal in the world.

I will sit in the (cozy) .... chair I can find.

That is the (bad) .... movie I have ever seen!

Digby's is the (new) .... restaurant in town.

FACTS

If an adjective has more than one syllable, the words "more" or "less" are used to form comparative adjectives. The words "most" or "least" are used to form superlative adjectives.

For each adjective, write one sentence using the comparative form and one sentence using the superlative form. Use either "more" and "most" or "less" and "least."

Interesting
Comparative: ....
Superlative: ....

Careful
Comparative: ....
Superlative: ....

Important
Comparative: ....
Superlative: ....

Frightening
Comparative: ....
Superlative: ....

Delicious
Comparative: ....
Superlative: ....

★ | Choosing Words

Writers look for words that will make their writing interesting and give more information.

Read the words in the word gallery. Choose two words from each set and write a sentence with the words. If you are not sure exactly what each word means, use a dictionary to find the meaning.

Instead of "good," use:

delightful   excellent   admirable

splendid   satisfying   talented

Instead of "bother," use:

annoy   pester   trouble

disturb   nag

....

....

....

....

....

Instead of "go," use:

flee   run   escape   plod   wander   scurry   roam

....

....

....

....

Similes

Similes are phrases that compare one thing to another using the words "like" or "as."

Complete the similes in each sentence using one of the words from the word bank.

| fish | honey | lion | mice | peacock | tack |

Justin swam like a ....

The thorns on the rose were as sharp as a ....

My dog thinks he is as powerful as a ....

You should be as proud as a .... of all the work you have done.

Let's be quiet like .... while the baby sleeps.

The poem that Sam wrote his mom for Mother's Day was as sweet as ....

★ Design a Poster

Advertisements use persuasive, descriptive words to convince people to act or think in a certain way.

Persuade people to visit your hometown. What words would you use to describe your city in a way that would make people want to take a trip there? What features does it have that are interesting? What kind of picture can you draw to let people see that it's a great place to stay? Write your ideas in the work space. Then design a tourist poster in the space below.

Work Space

Words that describe my hometown: ....
....
....
....
....

Why people should visit:

....
....
....
....
....
....

Why people should visit:

....
....
....
....
....
....

Diagrams can help a reader understand a concept. They often have labels that name various parts of the diagram.

Look at the diagram of the rain forest. Then answer the questions.

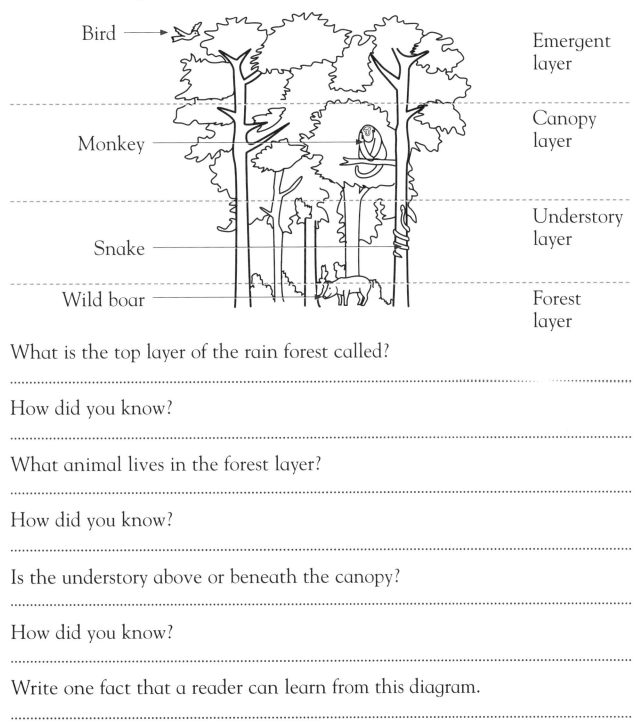

What is the top layer of the rain forest called?

....

How did you know?

....

What animal lives in the forest layer?

....

How did you know?

....

Is the understory above or beneath the canopy?

....

How did you know?

....

Write one fact that a reader can learn from this diagram.

....

Adverbs

An adverb describes a verb (an action or state of being). It tells how, where, when, how often, and why something is done.

In each sentence, underline the adverb. Then circle the verb it describes.

The fox ran quickly into its den.

I swallowed the medicine easily.

The actor performed well.

The patient rested comfortably in bed.

Theo accidentally tripped on the stairs.

I will read that book soon.

Sandra usually walks to school.

The soccer player never misses a practice.

The snake hid underground.

The class waited impatiently for the bell to ring.

A conjunction is a word that is used to join sentences, ideas, phrases, or words.

Choose the conjunction from the conjunction bank that best completes each sentence.

and	but	or	so	because	unless

We won't go to the baseball game _____ it stops raining.

Hannah is good at drawing, _____ she has won many drawing contests.

I like chocolate, _____ I prefer vanilla.

Dave forgot to put on sunscreen, _____ he got a sunburn.

Do your chores, _____ you won't get to play outside.

I am going to bed _____ I am tired.

Write three sentences using conjunctions.

....

....

....

★ Types of Conjunction

Coordinating conjunctions combine two equal words, phrases, or parts of sentences. Subordinating conjunctions combine two unequal words, phrases, or parts of sentences.

Use a coordinating conjunction to rewrite each pair of sentences as a single sentence.

and	or	so

Grandma is good at sewing. She will hem my pants.

....

Erin flies planes. Erin flies helicopters.

....

Lily wants to play checkers. Lily wants to play cards.

....

Use a subordinating conjunction to rewrite each pair of sentences as a single sentence.

after	because	unless

I bought red shoes. Red is my favorite color.

....

I am going to the playground. I finish my snack.

....

The dog won't bite you. You bother it.

....

Using a Dictionary

A dictionary gives information about words, such as spelling, meaning, part of speech, usage, and pronunciation.

Study the dictionary page. Then answer the questions.

merry
adjective
happy and cheerful.
Comparisons **merrier**,
merriest

mess
messes *noun*
things that are dirty
or in the wrong
place and look
untidy. *There was
a big* **mess** *after
they had finished
cooking.*
messy *adjective*

met
from the verb **to meet**.
I **met** *my friend in
town yesterday.*

metal
metals *noun*
a substance that is
found in rocks and
can be hammered or
stretched into a
shape. Iron, gold, and
copper are all metals.
*Heat can be passed
through metals.*
metallic *adjective*

meteorite
meteorites *noun*
a piece of rock that
falls to the Earth from
space without burning
up. *Pieces of rock that
burn up as they enter
the Earth's atmosphere
are called* **meteorites**.
say **meet**-ee-or-ite

microphone
microphones *noun*
a device used to send
sound over a distance
or to make it louder.

microscope
microscopes *noun*
an instrument that
magnifies very tiny
things so that they
can be seen in detail.

microwave oven
noun
an oven that cooks
food very quickly by
passing electrical
signals through it.

What is an example of a metal?

....

For the full definition of the word "met," what word would you look up?

....

Would that word be placed before this page or after this page?

....

Three entries on this page share a root word that means small.

    What are the three entries?   What is the root?

    ....

    ....

What is the adverb form of merry?

....

What are the comparative and superlative adjectives of messy?

....

★ Homographs

Homographs are words that share the same spelling but have different meanings.

Read each set of clues below to figure out the homograph.

The sound a telephone makes
Jewelry worn on the finger

....

Nearby
To shut something, such as a door or a box

....

To bend at the waist
A weapon made of bent wood and string

....

To rip
A liquid released from the eyes

....

The sound a dog makes
The outer part of a tree

....

Done in a good or satisfactory way
A deep hole in the ground from which water is taken

....

adwcskfbomhqanwscjgikeyz

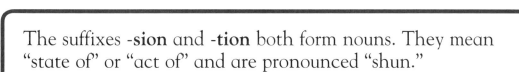

-ion Suffixes

The suffixes **-sion** and **-tion** both form nouns. They mean "state of" or "act of" and are pronounced "shun."

Write the base word for each word shown.

The "Shun" Mansion

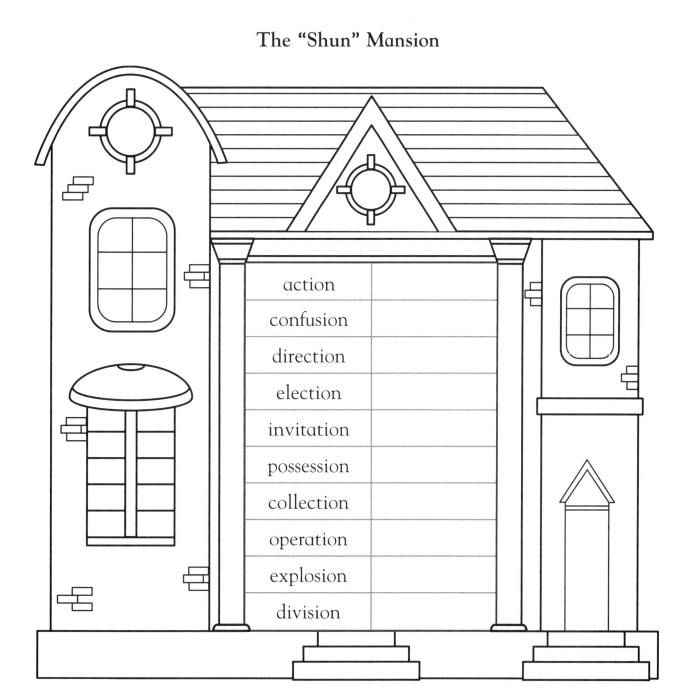

action	
confusion	
direction	
election	
invitation	
possession	
collection	
operation	
explosion	
division	

Clauses

FACTS

An independent clause can stand alone as a complete sentence.
A dependent clause cannot stand alone.

Determine whether each of the following is a dependent clause or an independent clause. Underline the correct answer.

When it snowed

dependent clause | **independent clause**

Cats purr

dependent clause | **independent clause**

If the train is late

dependent clause | **independent clause**

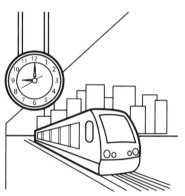

This book is funny

dependent clause | **independent clause**

A dependent clause and an independent clause can be joined to make a complete sentence called a complex sentence. Write an independent clause for each dependent clause to make a complete complex sentence.

When you hear the bell, ...

After Riley plays soccer, ...

Because Meg knows the way, ...

If I could fly, ...

Sentences can be simple, compound, or complex.

A simple sentence has one subject and one verb.
Write two simple sentences.

....

....

....

....

A compound sentence has two independent clauses joined by
a coordinating conjunction. Write two compound sentences.

....

....

....

....

A complex sentence has a dependent clause and an independent clause.
Write two complex sentences.

....

....

....

....

Write a Personal Narrative

Narrative writing tells a story. A personal narrative is written from your point of view and tells about your experiences.

Before you write, plan your narrative.

What event or experience will you write about?

....

When did it happen?

....

Where did it happen?

....

Write at least three interesting details about your topic.

....

....

....

What happened in the end?

....

Now that you have a plan, write your narrative on page 47 using the Personal Narrative Checklist:

✓ Use complete sentences.
✓ Use proper capitalization.
✓ Use correct punctuation.
✓ Use words that help tell the order of events: "first," "next," "then," and "finally."
✓ Spell all words correctly. Check a dictionary if you are not sure of a spelling.
✓ Use adjectives and adverbs to add interesting details to your writing.
✓ Use a variety of sentences: simple, compound, and complex.

Title: ....

By: ....

....

....

....

....

....

....

....

....

....

....

....

....

....

Certificate

3rd Grade

Congratulations to

....

for successfully
finishing this book.

GOOD JOB!

You're a star.

Date

....

Answer Section
with Parents' Notes

This workbook is a fun way to help your child build third-grade literacy skills. All of the activities support the Common Core English Language Arts Standards, a set of shared educational goals for each grade level currently used by 45 states, the District of Columbia, and four U.S. territories.

Contents

These activities are intended for a child to complete with adult support, as needed. The topics covered help children understand and make connections to the texts they read in school and on their own. The topics are:

- parts of speech: nouns, pronouns, verbs, adjectives, adverbs, prepositions, and conjunctions;
- types of words: compound words, abstract nouns, homophones, homographs;
- punctuation: quotation marks, apostrophes (possessives), apostrophes (contractions);
- sentence composition: subject and predicate, spelling, independent clauses and dependent clauses, simple, compound, and complex sentences;
- texts and text features: capitalizing titles, main idea and supporting details, point of view, cause and effect, infographics, dictionary;
- literature: myths and poetry;
- writing: letter writing, persuasive writing, personal narrative.

How to Help Your Child

These skills are a starting point for language arts awareness and instruction in your child's everyday life. To build language arts skills, provide access to a variety of fiction and nonfiction texts. Read together and discuss what you read. What words or ideas seem interesting or new to your child as you read together? What features of a text help make the text clearer? Why do writers write what they do, and how do they structure their writing?

This workbook gives children opportunities to work with a variety of different types of words and learn correct punctuation. Help children practice these skills by encouraging them to write letters to family members or favorite authors. Encourage children to write narratives about personal experiences by having them keep a journal. Celebrate our language with your child every day!

★ Compound Words

FACTS
Two words can be placed together to make one compound word.

Read the clues. Then unscramble the letters to reveal the compound word that answers the clue.

Joe's daughter's baby boy (nosndrag) __grandson__

Needs oars to move across water (wortoab) __rowboat__

Brown boxes may be made of this (darcdraob) __cardboard__

Red, orange, yellow, green, blue, violet, indigo (wbonair) __rainbow__

A place to dig and play (xbodans) __sandbox__

A sack for school supplies, carried on both shoulders (kacpkacb) __backpack__

Carries astronauts or aliens (pihescaps) __spaceship__

A bird that makes holes in trees (rekcepdoow) __woodpecker__

A sea creature with no bones (hsifyellj) __jellyfish__

Hot breakfast cereal (laemtoa) __oatmeal__

Encourage your child to find compound words in a newspaper or magazine article.

Abstract Nouns ★

FACTS
A concrete noun names something that can be recognized with the senses. An abstract noun names a concept that cannot be recognized with the senses.

Circle the fish that show abstract nouns.

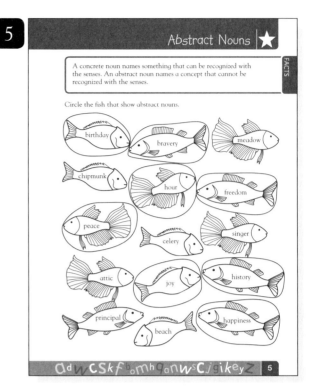

Ask your child to explain why the nouns that were not selected are not abstract nouns.

★ Sound-Alike Words

FACTS
Homophones are words that sound alike but have different spellings and meanings.

In each sentence, a pair of homophones is given. Underline the correct homophone to complete each sentence.

I am allowed / aloud to walk to the library alone.

Holly was to / too tired to go on the hike.

The dog's fir / fur was soft and silky.

Have you heard / herd the weather forecast?

A penny is worth one cent / sent.

If you put a lock on your bike, no one will steal / steel it.

There is not much traffic on our road / rode.

Our dog ate the hole / whole pie when we weren't looking.

The driver pressed the brake / break pedal to stop the car.

I knew / new how the movie ended before I saw it.

Homophones can be confusing, but the more your children work with the words and recognize homophones, the more they will recall the correct spelling for the context.

Capitalizing Titles ★

FACTS
Use capitalization for the first, last, and major words in titles.

Draw a line under the letters that should be capitalized in each book title.

the adventures of tom sawyer

alice in wonderland

little house on the prairie

the book of fables

big red

charlotte's web

a bear called paddington

the jungle book

the lion, the witch, and the wardrobe

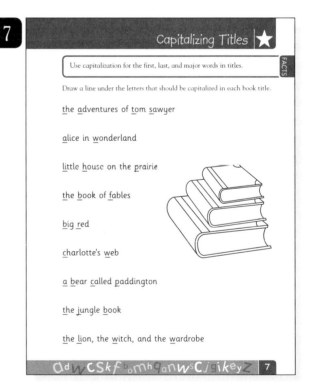

Go through a magazine with your child to demonstrate how capitalization is used in article titles. In some instances, all caps will be used in the design, but words may be set in uppercase and lowercase in the table of contents.

★ Myths

FACTS

Myths have been created by people of all cultures to explain their history and the ways of the world.

Read the myth, and then answer the questions.

Pandora's Box: A Greek Myth

Zeus, the king of all the Greek gods, was angry at Prometheus for giving the people of Earth fire without asking for his permission. Zeus asked Hephaestus, the god of craftsmanship, to make a beautiful woman from clay. Hephaestus made the woman, and she was named Pandora.

Zeus sent Pandora to live among the people of Earth as Prometheus's brother's wife. Before Pandora left, Zeus gave her a small, locked box. He made her promise never to open it. Zeus expected Prometheus and his brother to be so curious that they would want to open it.

Of course, Pandora was curious, too. The longer she held the box, the more unbearable it became not to know what was in it. Finally, Pandora could not stand it a moment longer. She opened the box.

Out flew all the evils now known to humanity. Crime, rage, disease, war, envy, and hatred came swarming out of the box. Pandora tried to contain them, but it was too late. They were out in the world.

Pandora cried out to her husband for help. They peered into the box together, and it was empty, except for one tiny, glowing creature. The creature climbed out of the box and flew away. That last creature was hope.

What does this myth explain?

It explains why there is evil in the world.

Why do you think the myth ends the way it does?

Answers may vary, but they should refer to the importance of hope.

If your child enjoys this myth, seek out a variety of myths from various cultures at your local library or online.

Character Profiles ★

FACTS

Characters in a story have their own unique traits, thoughts, feelings, and motivations.

Reread the story of Pandora's Box. Then complete the trading cards for two of the main characters in the story: Pandora and Zeus.

Greek Myth Trading Cards

Zeus

Zeus

Who he is: king of the Greek gods

Describe him in two words: Answers may vary

What he did: Answers may vary

Why he did what he did: Answers may vary

Pandora

Pandora

Who she is: a woman made by the gods

Describe her in two words: Answers may vary

What she did: Answers may vary

Why she did what she did: Answers may vary

While children's approaches to this activity will vary, make sure that the answers have an understandable relation to the text.

★ Writing a Letter

FACTS

Writing a letter is a great way to communicate information and ideas to another person or people. A letter is set up to show clearly whom the letter is from and when it was written.

Read about how to write a letter below.

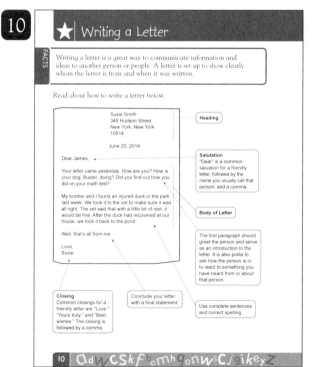

Susie Smith
345 Hudson Street
New York, New York
10014

June 20, 2014

Dear James,

Your letter came yesterday. How are you? How is your dog, Buster, doing? Did you find out how you did on your math test?

My brother and I found an injured duck in the park last week. We took it to the vet to make sure it was all right. The vet said that with a little bit of rest, it would be fine. After the duck had recovered at our house, we took it back to the pond.

Well, that's all from me.

Love,
Susie

Heading

Salutation
"Dear" is a common salutation for a friendly letter, followed by the name you usually call that person, and a comma.

Body of Letter

The first paragraph should greet the person and serve as an introduction to the letter. It is also polite to ask how the person is or to react to something you have heard from or about that person.

Conclude your letter with a final statement.

Use complete sentences and correct spelling

Closing
Common closings for a friendly letter are "Love," "Yours truly," and "Best wishes." The closing is followed by a comma.

Make sure your child understands the importance of placing the heading, salutation, and closing of a letter in the correct places on the page.

Writing a Letter ★

FACTS

A letter has a specific structure. A friendly letter would be written to family or friends.

Write a friendly letter to a friend or relative to share what you have been doing lately. Answers may vary

(Your name)

(Your street address)

(Your city, state, and zip code)

(Today's date)

(Your signature)

Ensure that your child has used complete sentences, correct spelling and punctuation, and has followed the template for the letter.

12

★ Verb Tenses

FACTS: A verb is a word that names an action or a state of being. Verbs can describe what is happening in the present, the past, and the future.

Underline the correct form of the verb for each sentence.

My mother drives / <u>will drive</u> me to school tomorrow.

I hear an owl hooted / <u>hooting</u> in the distance.

Charlie can <u>play</u> / played the tuba very well.

Jess <u>likes</u> / will like to write poetry, and she is very good at it.

The snake just slithering / <u>slithered</u> into the hollow log.

The teacher is <u>repeating</u> / repeated the directions for the students who are confused.

Look at Yoshi <u>dribble</u> / dribbled the basketball down the court!

I figure / <u>will figure</u> out the answers when I have time.

Maria deposits / <u>deposited</u> the money in the bank yesterday.

Liam <u>screamed</u> / will scream when he bang / <u>banged</u> his knee on the table.

Understanding verb tenses and other points of English grammar helps greatly when learning other languages.

13

Verb Tenses ★

FACTS: The different forms of a verb are called tenses.

Complete the table to describe the robot's activities. Write each verb shown in its other two tenses.

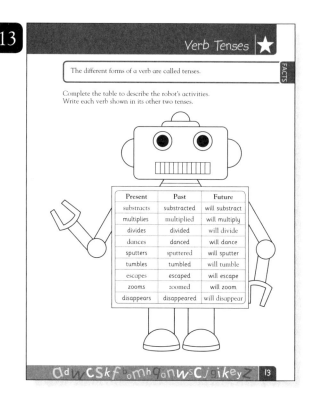

Present	Past	Future
substracts	subtracted	will subtract
multiplies	multiplied	will multiply
divides	divided	will divide
dances	danced	will dance
sputters	sputtered	will sputter
tumbles	tumbled	will tumble
escapes	escaped	will escape
zooms	zoomed	will zoom
disappears	disappeared	will disappear

Support your child's spelling, as necessary, in this activity.

14

★ Irregular Verbs

FACTS: With regular verbs, the past tense is formed by adding -ed to the end of the verb. Verbs that don't play by that rule are called irregular verbs.

The following verbs are irregular verbs written in the simple past tense. Write the present tense verb for each.

Past	Present
felt	feel
bet	bet
put	put
chose	choose
gave	give
swam	swim
left	leave
stung	sting
caught	catch

Write two versions of a sentence for each verb pair. Use the present tense in one and the simple past tense in the other. **Answers may vary**

rise/rose — I rise early. / I rose early.

sweep/swept — I sweep the floor. / I swept the floor.

sit/sat — I sit on a chair. / I sat on a chair.

bring/brought — I can bring snacks. / I brought snacks.

Encourage children to find more examples of irregular verbs in books or articles they read.

15

Quotation Marks ★

FACTS: When writing the words that people say, surround the words with quotation marks.

Place commas and quotation marks as needed in the following sentences.

"I will help you clean up," I said to my dad.

Jamie said, "I can't find my homework."

Max asked, "Do you want to ride bikes with me?"

"All you need is love," sang the Beatles.

The coach shouted, "Get into your positions!"

"My dog has fleas," sighed Ben.

"When is the next train to New York leaving?" I asked.

"Here I am!" I exclaimed.

"You need to floss your teeth every day," the dentist explained.

The teacher asked, "How many eggs are in a dozen?"

Errors in written language and punctuation are all around us. Spotting them and pointing them out can reinforce correct usage. A common mistake that people make is to use quotation marks to emphasize words. (I ate the "whole" pie.) If you spot an example of this, point it out to your child as an error.

★ Root Words

Some English words are formed from root words that come from ancient languages such as Greek and Latin.

Look at the illustrations. Each illustration shows a word made up of two root words. Find the root words in the root bank that make up each word. Write the word. Then write a definition for the word.

cycle (wheel, circle)	hemi (half)	uni (one)	phone (sound)
sphere (globe, ball)	tele (far, away)	thermo (heat)	meter (measure)

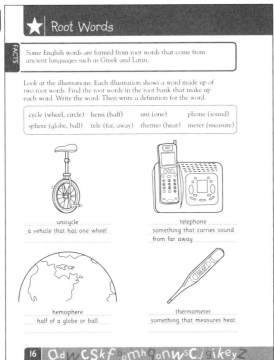

unicycle
a vehicle that has one wheel

telephone
something that carries sound from far away

hemisphere
half of a globe or ball

thermometer
something that measures heat

Encourage your child to think of more words that use the given roots. Write the words and have your child explain their meanings in the context of root words.

Main Idea and Supporting Details ★

The main idea is the most important information that the writer wants the reader to know. Main ideas are explained or proven with supporting details.

Read the paragraph. Write the main idea and three supporting details in the space provided.

All animals are different, but platypuses are particularly unusual animals. They look like a mixture of many other animals. They have flat tails like beavers. They have thick fur that is well suited to water like otters. They have bills and webbed feet like ducks. Their webbed feet have claws, so they are able to dig and to swim. Platypuses are also unusual because they are venomous mammals. A male platypus can sting other creatures to defend himself. Finally, platypuses are one of the only mammals that lays eggs.

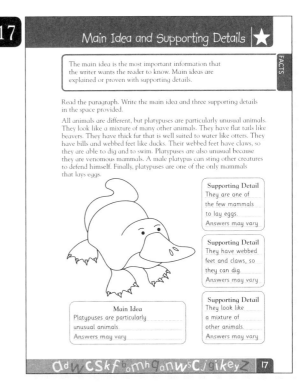

Supporting Detail
They are one of the few mammals to lay eggs.
Answers may vary

Supporting Detail
They have webbed feet and claws, so they can dig.
Answers may vary

Supporting Detail
They look like a mixture of other animals.
Answers may vary

Main Idea
Platypuses are particularly unusual animals.
Answers may vary

Finding main idea and supporting details is a key study skill that students will use throughout their school years. Answers will vary, but they should be understandable in relation to the text.

★ Myths

Myths have been created by people of all cultures to explain the history and the ways of the world.

The Heron and the Hummingbird: A Native American Myth

The birds Heron and Hummingbird both loved fish. They worried that there were not enough fish to satisfy them both. One day, Hummingbird said, "Let us race to the old tree at the end of the river. The bird who sits on top of the tree first will win. The winner of the race will own all the fish in the waters."

Heron agreed. The birds began their race the next day. The tree was a long way off, so they knew it would take some days to reach it. Heron moved slowly but steadily. His great wings made huge, quiet flaps. Quick little Hummingbird flew this way and that. He flew to all the pretty flowers he saw, stopping quickly to taste their nectar. If Heron got ahead of him, Hummingbird would zoom past him. By nightfall, Hummingbird was very tired. He fell asleep. Heron kept going, softly flapping his wings through the night.

This went on for three days and nights. When Hummingbird woke up on the fourth day, the tree was in sight. Heron was not, so Hummingbird excitedly zoomed ahead to win the race. When he arrived at the tree, he saw Heron sitting at the top. Heron had not stopped to sleep at all during the race. While Hummingbird was the faster flyer, he had stopped at too many flowers and taken too many naps.

From that day on, Heron has owned all the fish in the waters. Hummingbird could no longer fish, so he took his meals from the flowers he loved, stopping at each colorful blossom to sip its nectar.

Describe Heron. **Answers may vary**

Describe Hummingbird. **Answers may vary**

What does this myth explain? **Answers may vary**

If your child enjoys this myth, find other myths at your local library or online.

Point of View ★

The first person is written from the point of view of the main character or the author. The third person is told from the point of view of an outside observer.

Determine whether each passage below is written in the first person or the third person. Circle the correct answer.

Every fall, I am amazed when the leaves on the trees turn bright colors.

(first person)   third person

The bear curled up inside the hollow log. He got himself ready for the long, sleepy winter.

first person   (third person)

When I heard the alarm buzzing, I knew it was time to roll out of bed.

(first person)   third person

The barber asked Dan, "Just the usual cut today?" Dan wondered if he should try something new.

first person   (third person)

Write a sentence in the first person.   Answers may vary

Write a sentence in the third person.   Answers may vary

Check your child's sentences to ensure that the first-person sentence is written with "I" and that the third-person sentence is written from the point of view of an outside narrator.

20

★ Read a Historical Timeline

FACTS

A timeline shows the order of events in history.

Look at the timeline. Then answer the questions.

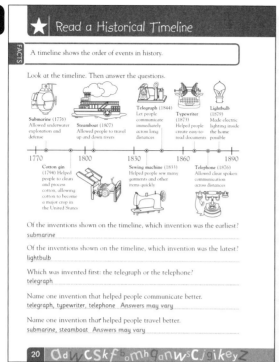

Submarine (1776) Allowed underwater exploration and defense

Steamboat (1807) Allowed people to travel up and down rivers

Telegraph (1844) Let people communicate immediately across long distances

Typewriter (1873) Helped people create easy-to-read documents

Lightbulb (1879) Made electric lighting inside the home possible

1770   1800   1830   1860   1890

Cotton gin (1794) Helped people to clean and process cotton, allowing cotton to become a major crop in the United States

Sewing machine (1833) Helped people sew many garments and other items quickly

Telephone (1876) Allowed clear spoken communication across distances

Of the inventions shown on the timeline, which invention was the earliest?
submarine

Of the inventions shown on the timeline, which invention was the latest?
lightbulb

Which was invented first: the telegraph or the telephone?
telegraph

Name one invention that helped people communicate better.
telegraph, typewriter, telephone Answers may vary

Name one invention that helped people travel better.
submarine, steamboat Answers may vary

20 adwCSkfᵇₒmhqanwˢCⱼgikeᵧZ

Encourage your child to create a timeline on any topic of particular interest.

21

Cause and Effect ★

FACTS

Cause is the reason something happens.
Effect is what happens as a result of the cause.

In each sentence, draw one line under the cause.
Draw two lines under the effect.

After <u>the phonograph was invented,</u> <u><u>people were able to listen to music at home.</u></u>

<u><u>The invention of the elevator</u></u> <u>allowed people to construct tall skyscrapers in cities.</u>

<u>Cleaning cotton by hand was a slow process,</u> and <u><u>many cotton seeds were lost.</u></u>

<u><u>Cotton could be cleaned quickly</u></u> with the <u>invention of the cotton gin.</u>

Write each cause and effect as one complete sentence.
Cause: People used to burn candles for light at home.
Effect: There were many house fires.
When people used to burn candles for light at home, there were many house fires. Answers may vary

Cause: People needed a safer source of light for their homes.
Effect: Thomas Edison worked on inventing the lightbulb.
People needed a safer source of light for their homes, so Thomas Edison worked on inventing the lightbulb. Answers may vary

Cause: Thomas Edison invented the lightbulb.
Effect: People could safely use electricity to light their homes.
After Thomas Edison invented the lightbulb, people could safely use electricity to light their homes. Answers may vary

adwCSkfᵇₒmhqanwˢCⱼgikeᵧZ 21

Children's sentences will vary, but a few examples are given.

22

★ Prefixes

FACTS

Adding a prefix to the beginning of a word changes the meaning of the orignal word.

Look at each set of words. Based on the meanings of the words, write what you think each prefix means.

agree   disagree
appear   disappear

Dis- means   not

read   misread
spell   misspell

Mis- means   wrong/wrongly

fill   refill
send   resend

Re- means   again

possible   impossible
proper   improper

Im- means   not

kindergarten   prekindergarten
historic   prehistoric

Pre- means   before

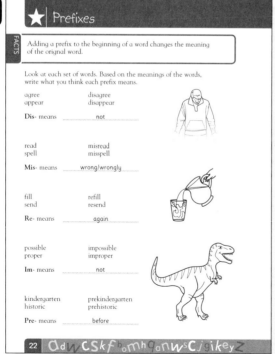

22 adwCSkfᵇₒmhqanwˢCⱼgikeᵧZ

Have your child talk out the answers before writing. For example, your child might say, "'Disagree' means 'not to agree,' and 'dislike' means 'not to like,' so 'dis' must mean 'not.'"

Suffixes ★

FACTS

Adding a suffix to the end of a word changes the meaning of the original word.

Look at each set of words. Based on the meanings of the words, write what you think each suffix means.

care   careful
pain   painful

-ful means   full of

care   careless
fear   fearless

-less means   without

bake   baker
teach   teacher

-er means   one who does something

low   lowest
high   highest

-est means   most

big   bigger
small   smaller

-er means   more

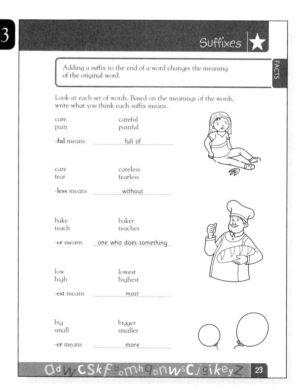

adwCSkfᵇₒmhqanwˢCⱼgikeᵧZ 23

Have your child talk out the answers before writing them. For example, your child might say, "'Careless' means 'without care,' and 'fearless' means 'without fear,' so 'less' must mean 'without.'"

★ Subject and Predicate

FACTS

The subject of a sentence tells who or what the sentence is about. The simple subject is usually a single noun. The predicate of a sentence tells what the subject is or does. The simple predicate is usually a single verb.

Draw one line under the subject of each sentence.
Draw two lines under the predicate of each sentence.
Circle the simple subject and the simple predicate.

(Erica) (knitted) a wool scarf.

My (grandfather) (collects) toy trains.

(Jason) (went) to the beach.

The fluffy (cat) (stretched) its legs.

(Minnesota) (has) many lakes.

The crooked (swing) (hangs) from the tree.

The jolly (farmer) (sang) while he worked.

The soccer (fans) (shouted) loudly when their team scored.

(Sally Ride) (was) the first American woman in space.

The (capital) of Colorado (is) (Denver).

Be sure your child is comfortable with this concept before moving on to the next activity.

25

Subject and Predicate ★

FACTS

Sometimes a sentence can have a compound subject, or more than one subject. A sentence can also have a compound predicate.

Read each sentence. Determine whether the underlined part of each sentence is a compound subject or a compound predicate. Some sentences have both! Circle the correct answer.

John and Tara enjoy swimming in the summer.

(Compound subject) | Compound predicate | Both

Mary opened her locker and looked for her science book.

Compound subject | (Compound predicate) | Both

The train will stop in Philadelphia and continue on to Baltimore.

Compound subject | (Compound predicate) | Both

Tom and his dad went fishing in the creek.

(Compound subject) | Compound predicate | Both

Jack and Mary spoke with the teacher and the principal.

(Compound subject) | Compound predicate | Both

Birds and butterflies are pretty to see and help flowers grow.

Compound subject | Compound predicate | (Both)

The actors and the dancers performed wonderfully and made the audience clap and cheer.

Compound subject | Compound predicate | (Both)

For fun, have your child compose a wacky sentence with long compound subjects and predicates.

26

★ Read a Poem

FACTS

Poems are made up of lines. Lines grouped together in a poem are called a stanza.

Read the poem. Then answer the questions. Answers may vary

Little Things
By Ebenezer Cobham Brewer

Little drops of water,
Little grains of sand,
Make the mighty ocean
And the pleasant land.

Thus the little minutes,
Humble though they be,
Make the mighty ages
Of eternity.

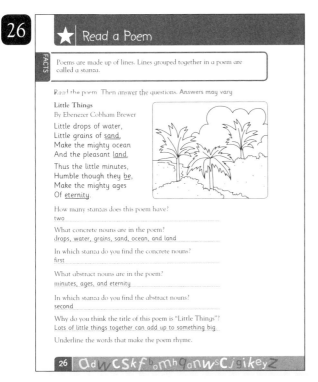

How many stanzas does this poem have?
two

What concrete nouns are in the poem?
drops, water, grains, sand, ocean, and land

In which stanza do you find the concrete nouns?
first

What abstract nouns are in the poem?
minutes, ages, and eternity

In which stanza do you find the abstract nouns?
second

Why do you think the title of this poem is "Little Things"?
Lots of little things together can add up to something big.

Underline the words that make the poem rhyme.

Look in your local library for more poems to read with your child. Poetry will be found among the 800s in your library.

Write a Poem ★

FACTS

Poems are pleasing to the ear. They can be written with rhythm and rhyme.

Try writing an eight-line poem of your own. It can be about anything you like: a feeling, something in nature, or a favorite activity or pet. Use the structure of the poem "Little Things" on page 26.

Title: Answers may vary

Answers may vary

Children's poems will vary. Encourage children to read poems aloud so you can all hear them. Provide feedback and suggestions for improving poems.

Page 28

Apostrophes

Apostrophes can be used to show possession.

Read the passage. Add apostrophes for possession where they are needed.

Sarah's cat had three kittens. As Sarah stroked the kittens' soft heads, she thought, "How will I find homes for all of my cat's kittens?"

Sarah made posters to put up in her neighborhood. She also hung some in her friend Lindsay's neighborhood.

Lindsay's dad, Mr. Smith, called Sarah. "Next weekend is my brother's birthday," he said. "He has agreed that a kitten would be a wonderful present."

Sarah was happy to find a home for one of the kittens. She lifted a gray-and-white kitten out of its basket. She walked with it to the Smiths' house.

Later, Sarah's neighbor called. "Our house has been lonely since my husband's dog ran away," she said. "We would love to take two kittens."

The kittens' new homes were perfect.
Everyone was happy.

One of the most common mistakes people make with an apostrophe is "its"/"it's." Go over the difference between the two words with your child. You might even come up with your own strategy to recall which one gets the apostrophe! (The contraction for "it is" gets the apostrophe.)

Page 29

Apostrophes

Apostrophes are used when making contractions. A contraction takes two words and forms them into one.

Make contractions from the underlined words.

I would like to go home.	I'd
Susan cannot figure out how to use her MP3 player.	can't
I think you will like this movie.	you'll
My dog does not come when he is called.	doesn't
I would have taken the bus, but I missed it.	would've
It is going to snow later today.	it's
We are paddling in a canoe.	we're
Here is the cake I baked!	here's
You must not make noise when the baby is sleeping.	mustn't
You have got spinach in your teeth.	you've
They are not following the directions.	aren't
They are not following the directions.	They're

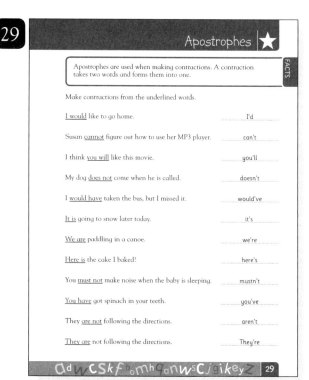

Check to make sure that your child has spelled each contraction correctly.

Page 30

Silent Consonants

Some consonants are silent in the spelling of a word. They are written, but not pronounced.

Meet the silent consonants. You'll never know they're there, unless you know how to spell the word. Match the words from the word bank to each silent consonant. Write the matching words on each silent consonant's briefcase. **Hint**: One word has two silent consonants.

write	neighbor	plumber	right	straight	knight	knife
	crumb	knot	wrong	thumb	who	
knee	doubt	high	dough	wrist	lamb	know

silent B   **silent GH**   **silent K**   **silent W**

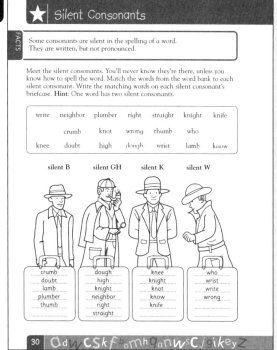

silent B: crumb, doubt, lamb, plumber, thumb
silent GH: dough, high, knight, neighbor, right, straight
silent K: knee, knight, knot, know, knife
silent W: who, wrist, write, wrong

Make a game out of finding silent consonants on signs as you walk or drive around town.

Page 31

Look-Say-Cover-Write-Check

A great way to learn how to spell words is the look-say-cover-write-check method.

Look at the words. Say the words aloud. Cover the words. Then write the words. Check your work against the word list.

Word	First Try	Second Try	Third Try
blueberries			
cheapest			
climber			
delightful			
discover			
earring			
fairly			
neighbor			
rewrite			
safer			
scarecrow			
shadow			
telephone			
wireless			
wreck			

Answers may vary

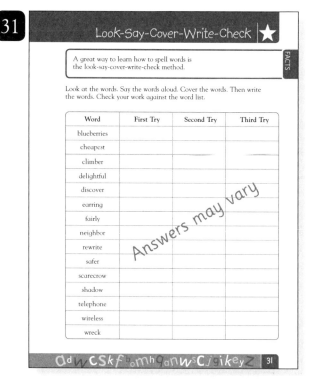

Have your child say the words aloud and check the work. Make connections to other pages in the workbook. Do any of these words contain prefixes or suffixes? Silent consonants? Which words are nouns, verbs, adjectives, and adverbs? Are any compound words? What are the roots of the words?

★ Adjectives

FACTS
To compare two nouns, you can use a comparative adjective. When comparing more than two nouns, you can use a superlative adjective.

Write the comparative form of the adjectives.

The Missouri River is (long) __longer__ than the Mississippi River.

The drums were (loud) __louder__ than the other instruments in the band.

I feel (good) __better__ than I did when I woke up this morning.

My cat's fur is (soft) __softer__ than my dog's fur.

Your joke is (silly) __sillier__ than the one I told.

Winter seems (dark) __darker__ than any other season.

The book I just read has a (happy) __happier__ ending than the last book I read.

Write the superlative form of the adjectives.

My uncle is the (tall) __tallest__ member of my family.

Robert is the (quiet) __quietest__ child in the class.

Ms. Gray is the (busy) __busiest__ person I know.

The blue whale is the (large) __largest__ animal in the world.

I will sit in the (cozy) __coziest__ chair I can find.

That is the (bad) __worst__ movie I have ever seen!

Digby's is the (new) __newest__ restaurant in town.

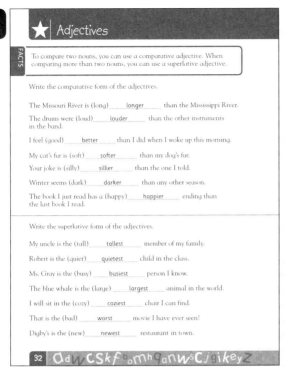

Demonstrate how to use comparative and superlative adjectives in everyday conversation.

Adjectives ★

FACTS
If an adjective has more than one syllable, the words "more" or "less" are used to form comparative adjectives. The words "most" or "least" are used to form superlative adjectives.

For each adjective, write one sentence using the comparative form and one sentence using the superlative form. Use either "more" and "most" or "less" and "least."

Answers may vary. For reference, the comparative and superlative forms of each adjective are given below.

Interesting
Comparative: _more interesting; less interesting_
Superlative: _most interesting; least interesting_

Careful
Comparative: _more careful; less careful_
Superlative: _most careful; least careful_

Important
Comparative: _more important; less important_
Superlative: _most important; least important_

Frightening
Comparative: _more frightening; less frightening_
Superlative: _most frightening; least frightening_

Delicious
Comparative: _more delicious; less delicious_
Superlative: _most delicious; least delicious_

Children's sentences will vary. For reference, the comparative and superlative form of each adjective is given. Check to make sure that your child is using the correct form when creating sentences.

★ Choosing Words

FACTS
Writers look for words that will make their writing interesting and give more information.

Read the words in the word gallery. Choose two words from each set and write a sentence with the words. If you are not sure exactly what each word means, use a dictionary to find the meaning.

Instead of "good," use:
delightful   excellent   admirable
splendid   satisfying   talented

Answers may vary

Instead of "bother," use:
annoy   pester   trouble
disturb   nag

Answers may vary

Instead of "go," use:
flee   run   escape   plod   wander   scurry   roam

Answers may vary

Check your child's sentences to ensure proper spelling, punctuation, and word usage.

Similes ★

FACTS
Similes are phrases that compare one thing to another using the words "like" or "as."

Complete the similes in each sentence using one of the words from the word bank.

fish   honey   lion   mice   peacock   tack

Justin swam like a __fish__.

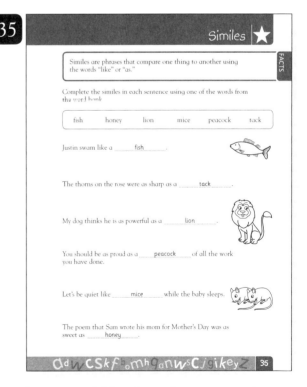

The thorns on the rose were as sharp as a __tack__.

My dog thinks he is as powerful as a __lion__.

You should be as proud as a __peacock__ of all the work you have done.

Let's be quiet like __mice__ while the baby sleeps.

The poem that Sam wrote his mom for Mother's Day was as sweet as __honey__.

Invite your child to play with creating similes.

36

Design a Poster

FACTS

Advertisements use persuasive, descriptive words to convince people to act or think in a certain way.

Persuade people to visit your hometown. What words would you use to describe your city in a way that would make people want to take a trip there? What features does it have that are interesting? What kind of picture can you draw to let people see that it's a great place to stay? Write your ideas in the work space. Then design a tourist poster in the space below.

Work Space

Words that describe my hometown: Answers may vary

Why people should visit:
Answers may vary

Why people should visit:
Answers may vary

Answers may vary

Work with your child to brainstorm ideas for the poster. Ensure that the writing is vivid and persuasive.

37

Read a Diagram

FACTS

Diagrams can help a reader understand a concept. They often have labels that name various parts of the diagram.

Look at the diagram of the rain forest. Then answer the questions.

What is the top layer of the rain forest called?
emergent layer

How did you know?
There is a label naming the topmost layer.

What animal lives in the forest layer?
wild boar

How did you know?
The picture shows a wild boar in the forest layer. Both have labels.

Is the understory above or beneath the canopy?
beneath

How did you know?
The picture shows each layer's position. The labels name the layers.

Write one fact that a reader can learn from this diagram.
Answers may vary

Have your child talk through the answers to the questions before writing them down. Discuss how your child arrived at each answer.

38

Adverbs

FACTS

An adverb describes a verb (an action or state of being). It tells how, where, when, how often, and why something is done.

In each sentence, underline the adverb. Then circle the verb it describes.

The fox (ran) <u>quickly</u> into its den.

I (swallowed) the medicine <u>easily</u>.

The actor (performed) <u>well</u>.

The patient (rested) <u>comfortably</u> in bed.

Theo <u>accidentally</u> (tripped) on the stairs.

I will (read) that book <u>soon</u>.

Sandra <u>usually</u> (walks) to school.

The soccer player <u>never</u> (misses) a practice.

The snake (hid) <u>underground</u>.

The class (waited) <u>impatiently</u> for the bell to ring.

Ask your child to explain why a writer would want to use adverbs.

39

Conjunctions

FACTS

A conjunction is a word that is used to join sentences, ideas, phrases, or words.

Choose the conjunction from the conjunction bank that best completes each sentence.

and but or so because unless

We won't go to the baseball game unless it stops raining.

Hannah is good at drawing, and she has won many drawing contests.

I like chocolate, but I prefer vanilla.

Dave forgot to put on sunscreen, so he got a sunburn.

Do your chores, or you won't get to play outside.

I am going to bed because I am tired.

Write three sentences using conjunctions.

Answers may vary

Answers may vary

Answers may vary

Check the sentences to ensure that conjunctions are used correctly.

★ Types of Conjunction

FACTS

Coordinating conjunctions combine two equal words, phrases, or parts of sentences. Subordinating conjunctions combine two unequal words, phrases, or parts of sentences.

Use a coordinating conjunction to rewrite each pair of sentences as a single sentence.

and	or	so

Grandma is good at sewing. She will hem my pants.
Grandma is good at sewing, so she will hem my pants.

Erin flies planes. Erin flies helicopters.
Erin flies planes and helicopters.

Lily wants to play checkers. Lily wants to play cards.
Lily wants to play checkers or cards.

Use a subordinating conjunction to rewrite each pair of sentences as a single sentence.

after	because	unless

I bought red shoes. Red is my favorite color.
I bought red shoes because red is my favorite color.

I am going to the playground. I finish my snack.
I am going to the playground after I finish my snack.

The dog won't bite you. You bother it.
The dog won't bite you unless you bother it.

Make sure that your child has used all conjunctions correctly. Come up with other sentences where your child can practice using conjunctions.

Using a Dictionary ★

FACTS

A dictionary gives information about words, such as spelling, meaning, part of speech, usage, and pronunciation.

Study the dictionary page. Then answer the questions.

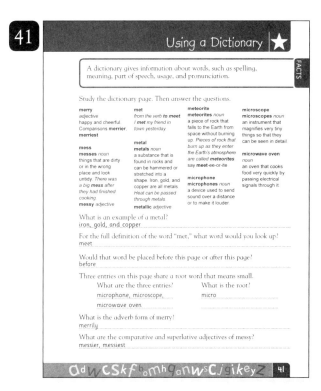

merry
adjective
happy and cheerful.
Comparisons **merrier**, **merriest**

mess
messes *noun*
things that are dirty or in the wrong place and look untidy. *There was a big mess after they had finished cooking.*
messy *adjective*

met
from the verb **to meet**
I met my friend in town yesterday

metal
metals *noun*
a substance that is found in rocks and can be hammered or stretched into a shape. Iron, gold, and copper are all metals. *Heat can be passed through metals.*
metallic *adjective*

meteorite
meteorites *noun*
a piece of rock that falls to the Earth from space without burning up. *Pieces of rock that burn up as they enter the Earth's atmosphere are called meteorites.*
say **meet**-ee-or-ite

microphone
microphones *noun*
a device used to send sound over a distance or to make it louder.

microscope
microscopes *noun*
an instrument that magnifies very tiny things so that they can be seen in detail.

microwave oven
noun
an oven that cooks food very quickly by passing electrical signals through it

What is an example of a metal?
iron, gold, and copper

For the full definition of the word "met," what word would you look up?
meet

Would that word be placed before this page or after this page?
before

Three entries on this page share a root word that means small.
What are the three entries?   What is the root?
microphone, microscope,   micro
microwave oven

What is the adverb form of merry?
merrily

What are the comparative and superlative adjectives of messy?
messier, messiest

Encourage your child to use a dictionary to look up words that are new or unclear. Demonstrate how you use a dictionary.

★ Homographs

FACTS

Homographs are words that share the same spelling but have different meanings.

Read each set of clues below to figure out the homograph.

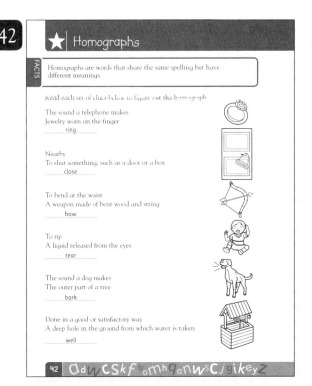

The sound a telephone makes
Jewelry worn on the finger
ring

Nearby
To shut something, such as a door or a box
close

To bend at the waist
A weapon made of bent wood and string
bow

To rip
A liquid released from the eyes
tear

The sound a dog makes
The outer part of a tree
bark

Done in a good or satisfactory way
A deep hole in the ground from which water is taken
well

Have your child say each homograph pair aloud. Notice that homographs are not always pronounced in the same way. Homograph simply means "same spelling."

-ion Suffixes ★

FACTS

The suffixes **-sion** and **-tion** both form nouns. They mean "state of" or "act of" and are pronounced "shun."

Write the base word for each word shown.

The "Shun" Mansion

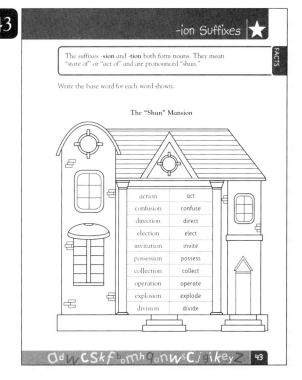

action	act
confusion	confuse
direction	direct
election	elect
invitation	invite
possession	possess
collection	collect
operation	operate
explosion	explode
division	divide

The word "mansion" is shown, but your child is not asked to decode its base word. "Mansion" is derived from a Latin root word meaning "dwelling."

★ Clauses

FACTS
An independent clause can stand alone as a complete sentence.
A dependent clause cannot stand alone.

Determine whether each of the following is a dependent clause
or an independent clause. Underline the correct answer.

When it snowed
<u>dependent clause</u> | independent clause

Cats purr
dependent clause | <u>independent clause</u>

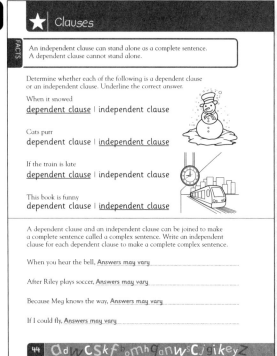

If the train is late
<u>dependent clause</u> | independent clause

This book is funny
dependent clause | <u>independent clause</u>

A dependent clause and an independent clause can be joined to make
a complete sentence called a complex sentence. Write an independent
clause for each dependent clause to make a complete complex sentence.

When you hear the bell, **Answers may vary**

After Riley plays soccer, **Answers may vary**

Because Meg knows the way, **Answers may vary**

If I could fly, **Answers may vary**

Check to ensure that your child writes
an independent clause and that the words
are spelled correctly. Also be sure that
the sentence is properly punctuated.
Provide support as necessary.

Types of Sentences ★

FACTS
Sentences can be simple, compound, or complex.

A simple sentence has one subject and one verb.
Write two simple sentences.

Answers may vary

Answers may vary

A compound sentence has two independent clauses joined by
a coordinating conjunction. Write two compound sentences.

Answers may vary

Answers may vary

A complex sentence has a dependent clause and an independent clause.
Write two complex sentences.

Answers may vary

Answers may vary

Check to ensure that your child is writing
complete sentences and that the words are
spelled correctly. Also be sure the sentences
are properly punctuated.

★ Write a Personal Narrative

FACTS
Narrative writing tells a story. A personal narrative is written from
your point of view and tells about your experiences.

Before you write, plan your narrative.
What event or experience will you write about?
Answers may vary

When did it happen?   Where did it happen?
Answers may vary   **Answers may vary**

Write at least three interesting details about your topic.
Answers may vary

Answers may vary

Answers may vary

What happened in the end?
Answers may vary

Now that you have a plan, write your narrative on page 47 using
the Personal Narrative Checklist:

✓ Use complete sentences.
✓ Use proper capitalization.
✓ Use correct punctuation.
✓ Use words that help tell the order of events: "first," "next," "then,"
   and "finally."
✓ Spell all words correctly. Check a dictionary if you are not sure of
   a spelling.
✓ Use adjectives and adverbs to add interesting details to your writing.
✓ Use a variety of sentences: simple, compound, and complex.

Your child might want to write a draft of
a personal narrative on a separate piece of paper
before writing a final draft on page 47. Work with
your child to make sure that the narrative flows
in a logical order.

Write a Personal Narrative ★

Title: **Answers may vary**

By: **Answers may vary**

Answers may vary

Help children review their writing by comparing
the text to the rubric on page 46.